KEY QUESTIONS
in AMERICAN HISTORY

DID THE CIVIL RIGHTS MOVEMENT ACHIEVE CIVIL RIGHTS?

SIYAVUSH SAIDIAN

PowerKiDS
press
New York

Published in 2019 by The Rosen Publishing Group, Inc.
29 East 21st Street, New York, NY 10010

First Edition

Editor: Elizabeth Krajnik
Book Design: Tanya Dellaccio

Photo Credits: Cover, back cover, pp. 1, 3–32 (background) Tatiana Kasyanova/Shutterstock.com; cover, back cover, pp. 5, 6, 11, 12, 15, 27 (newspaper clipping) STILLFX/Shutterstock.com; cover (March on Washington) Robert W. Kelley/The LIFE Picture Collection/Getty Images; cover (Martin Luther King Jr.) Consolidated News Pictures/Getty Images; cover (Malcom X) Truman Moore/The LIFE Images Collection/Getty Images; p. 5 (top) https://commons.wikimedia.org/wiki/File:Lyndon_Johnson_meeting_with_civil_rights_leaders.jpg; p. 5 (bottom) Charles Shaw/Archive Photos/Getty Images; p. 7 (top) Tupungato/Shutterstock.com; p. 7 (bottom) Everett Historical/Shutterstock.com; p. 9 (top) Historical/Corbis Historical/Getty Images; p. 9 (bottom) https://en.wikipedia.org/wiki/File:Joseph_Rainey_-_Brady-Handy.jpg; pp. 11 (top), 13 (bottom), 17 (Medgar Evers), 25 (bottom) Hulton Archive/Getty Images; p. 11 (bottom) https://commons.wikimedia.org/wiki/File:President_Rutherford_Hayes_1870_-_1880_Restored.jpg; p. 13 (top) Baltimore Sun/Tribune News Service/Getty Images; p. 15 (top) Carl Iwasaki/The LIFE Images Collection/Getty Images; p. 15 (bottom) William Lovelace/Hulton Archive/Getty Images; p. 16 https://commons.wikimedia.org/wiki/File:Booker_T_Washington_retouched_flattened-crop.jpg; p. 17 (W. E. B. DuBois) https://commons.wikimedia.org/wiki/File:WEB_DuBois_1918.jpg; pp. 17 (Martin Luther King Jr.), 29 AFP/Getty Images; p. 19 (both) Shel Hershorn - HA/Inactive/Archive Photos/Getty Images; pp. 21 (top), 25 (top) Bettmann/Getty Images; p. 21 (bottom) https://commons.wikimedia.org/wiki/File:Rosaparks.jpg; p. 22 Courtesy of the Library of Congress; p. 23 https://commons.wikimedia.org/wiki/File:Malcolm_X_NYWTS_2a.jpg; p. 26 Ververidis Vasilis/Shutterstock.com; p. 27 Getty Images Entertainment/Getty Images North America/Getty Images.

Cataloging-in-Publication Data

Names: Saidian, Siyavush.
Title: Did the Civil Rights Movement achieve civil rights? / Siyavush Saidian.
Description: New York : PowerKids Press, 2019. | Series: Key questions in American history | Includes index.
Identifiers: LCCN ISBN 9781508167563 (pbk.) | ISBN 9781508167549 (library bound) | ISBN 9781508167570 (6 pack)
Subjects: LCSH: African Americans–Civil rights–History–Juvenile literature. | Civil rights movements–United States–History–20th century–Juvenile literature. | United States–Race relations–Juvenile literature.
Classification: LCC E185.61 S23 2019 | DDC 323.1196'073–dc23

Manufactured in the United States of America

CPSIA Compliance Information: Batch CS18PK: For Further Information contact Rosen Publishing, New York, New York at 1-800-237-9932

CONTENTS

CIVIL RIGHTS AND WRONGS

The Voting Rights Act of 1965, signed by President Lyndon B. Johnson, is rightly treated as one of the most important pieces of civil rights **legislation** passed in the 20th century. Under this law, African Americans and other **minorities** are guaranteed the right to vote, and the government is prevented from **discriminating** against people to take away this right.

The main supporters of the Voting Rights Act were members of the civil rights movement, which rose to popularity in the 1950s. Led by Martin Luther King Jr., this movement fought for an end to discrimination. Despite the successes of the civil rights movement, racism and discrimination still exist in the United States. This has caused some historians, politicians, and **activists** to question whether the civil rights movement truly achieved its goals.

MARTIN LUTHER KING JR., PRESIDENT LYNDON B. JOHNSON, AND MANY CIVIL RIGHTS ACTIVISTS PLAYED IMPORTANT ROLES IN THE CIVIL RIGHTS MOVEMENT.

HISTORIC MOMENTS

Even though the 15th and 24th **Amendments** were written to protect minority voting rights, laws prevented millions of African Americans from voting until 1965. Voting issues still continue today.

A CONFLICTED PAST

Some of the darkest moments in American history have revolved around the **institution** of slavery. Slavery came to the Americas during the 1500s. Over time, it became common in the colonies and then the United States. Later, the northern states became more industrial, relying on factories and machines, and banned slavery. The South, however, continued to depend on slave labor on farms and plantations.

Slavery was one of the most divisive issues in the 19th-century United States, and it eventually led to the start of the Civil War in 1861. Thousands of people died over the four years of the war. And for nearly a century after the conflict—and slavery—ended, African Americans still rarely had a voice in the local, state, or federal governments.

HISTORIC MOMENTS

Traders brought the first Africans to the British colonies in North America. The first slaves may have arrived in Jamestown, Virginia, in 1619.

THE FIRST PRESIDENT OF CIVIL RIGHTS

President Abraham Lincoln is widely respected as one of the nation's greatest leaders. He won the presidential election of 1860 in part by showing that the Republican Party was united and revealing the disunion of the Democratic Party. On January 1, 1863, Lincoln issued his final **Emancipation** Proclamation, which legally freed slaves in parts of the country under Confederate control. For this political action, he is often referred to as the Great Emancipator.

THE IMAGE BELOW SHOWS PRESIDENT ABRAHAM LINCOLN READING THE EMANCIPATION PROCLAMATION TO HIS CABINET.

AFTER THE WAR

The 12-year period after the Civil War ended is called Reconstruction. The purpose of Reconstruction was not only to reunite the former Confederate states with the Union but also to help African Americans and fix the problems caused by slavery in the South. During this time, some African Americans experienced opportunities made possible by their newfound freedom. However, the laws that protected minorities from discrimination were often only enforced because the South was occupied by Union soldiers to make sure white Confederates didn't come back into power.

During Reconstruction, some southern African Americans were elected to positions of power in the local, state, and federal governments. As a result, greater equality continued to spread and discrimination gradually decreased. In the late 1870s, however, Reconstruction came to an end.

HIRAM REVELS
FIRST BLACK SENATOR
IN THE UNITED STATES

JOSEPH
HAYNE
RAINEY

ELECTED IN 1870, JOSEPH HAYNE RAINEY WAS THE FIRST AFRICAN AMERICAN TO SERVE IN THE U.S. HOUSE OF REPRESENTATIVES.

ANOTHER DARK AGE

Most southerners were upset by the results of the Civil War. Many politicians tried everything they could to end Reconstruction. Riots and protests spread across the former Confederate states in the 1870s and, in 1877, this era of increased equality came to an end.

After 1877, southern states introduced a series of racist policies that became known as Jim Crow laws. Some of these laws stopped African Americans from voting by requiring literacy, or reading and writing, tests. Because many African Americans at the time were poor and had little education, they couldn't pass these tests. Other Jim Crow laws promoted **segregation**, which affected public transportation, schools, parks, and businesses.

RUTHERFORD B. HAYES WAS THE 19TH PRESIDENT OF THE UNITED STATES. BEFORE HE WAS ELECTED IN 1876, HE PROMISED TO REMOVE FEDERAL TROOPS FROM FORMER CONFEDERATE STATES, WHICH ALLOWED WHITE DEMOCRATS TO COME BACK INTO POWER.

CHANGING POLITICS

Even though the names of America's two most powerful political parties—the Democratic Party and the Republican Party—remain the same, a lot has changed since they were formed. Over the years, and for many reasons, the parties of the Civil War era swapped names. Today, the political beliefs of these earlier Democrats are closer to those of modern Republicans and those of these earlier Republicans are closer to those of modern Democrats.

RUTHERFORD B. HAYES

HISTORIC MOMENTS

Jim Crow laws got their name from a popular minstrel show act called *Jump Jim Crow*. Minstrel shows were performances in which white people pretended to be people of color in a racist way that was meant to be funny.

BEGINNINGS OF CHANGE

After the turn of the 20th century, a number of outspoken and powerful politicians and activists began fighting for greater racial equality in the United States. This led to the establishment of the National Association for the Advancement of Colored People (NAACP) in 1909. The NAACP's mission is to end segregation and discrimination. Throughout World War I, the Great Depression, and World War II, African Americans began gathering support for a major push for equal rights.

President Franklin D. Roosevelt supported the NAACP through some of his New Deal programs, but the push for racial equality was slowed after World War II. Although many people supported the African American leaders who fought for better treatment, it was difficult for everyone to agree on the best course of action.

HISTORIC MOMENTS

Beginning during World War I and continuing until the 1970s, the Great Migration saw more than 6 million African Americans leave the South to escape racism and find opportunities in urban areas in the North and West.

THE NAACP HAS BEEN FIGHTING FOR CIVIL RIGHTS SINCE 1909. THE ORGANIZATION WORKS TO EDUCATE AFRICAN AMERICANS ON THEIR RIGHTS AND MAKE SURE THAT ALL PEOPLE'S RIGHTS ARE HONORED REGARDLESS OF RACE.

THE SAME OLD DEAL?

Some of President Roosevelt's New Deal programs were successful, including those aimed at helping African Americans. Millions received loans, jobs, or other relief during the Great Depression thanks to New Deal programs. However, there were still discriminatory and racist practices in place in the U.S. government despite Roosevelt's best efforts at reducing them. The Federal Housing Administration provided housing targeted at white middle-class and lower-middle-class families, which left lower-class African American families living in less desirable situations.

FRANKLIN D. ROOSEVELT

FIGHTING FOR RIGHTS

Empowered by the support of President Roosevelt and the NAACP, the civil rights movement fought for greater racial equality. Countless people took to the streets of America to protest the injustices that were harming the country. However, there was still strong **opposition** to the movement, especially in the South.

Civil rights leaders fought hard for everything they gained in the 1950s and 1960s. Some police, politicians, and organizations that were committed to maintaining discrimination—including the Ku Klux Klan (KKK), the most famous white supremacy group—opposed them. No matter who stood against them, however, these civil rights leaders remained strong and continued to fight for equality.

HISTORIC MOMENTS

One of the greatest civil rights victories of the 20th century was the *Brown v. Board of Education of Topeka* ruling, which happened in 1954. In this legal case, the Supreme Court ruled that segregation in public schools is illegal and unconstitutional.

THE IMAGE BELOW SHOWS MARTIN LUTHER KING JR. AND HIS WIFE CORETTA SCOTT KING LEADING A BLACK VOTING RIGHTS MARCH FROM SELMA TO MONTGOMERY, ALABAMA.

HEROES AND LEADERS

The early days of the civil rights movement produced many great leaders, including W. E. B. Du Bois and Booker T. Washington. Du Bois, one of the founders of the NAACP, worked toward the immediate improvement of race relations and African American rights. Washington, however, worked toward advancing African Americans' economic position without challenging Jim Crow laws. Both men gained thousands of followers in the early 1900s despite their different viewpoints.

Beginning in the 1950s, more African American leaders came into the spotlight. Among them were Medgar Evers, a NAACP field officer and civil rights activist, and the most famous U.S. civil rights activist, Martin Luther King Jr. Both of these men were killed, but not before they encouraged millions of their fellow Americans to stand up to racial discrimination and fight for equal rights.

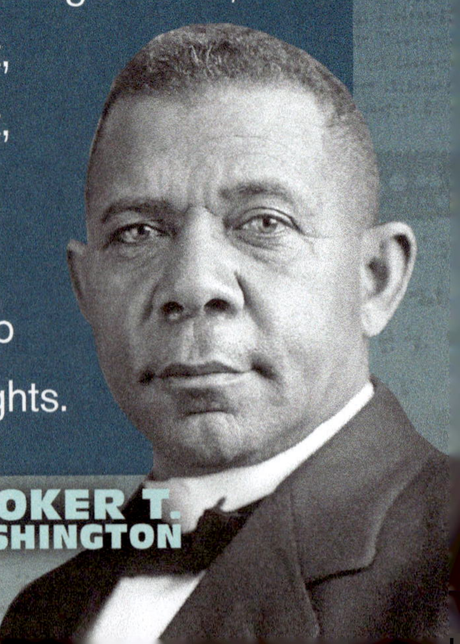
BOOKER T. WASHINGTON

W. E .B. DUBOIS

MEDGAR EVERS

MARTIN LUTHER KING JR. BECAME INTERESTED IN FIGHTING FOR EQUAL RIGHTS FOR HIS FELLOW AFRICAN AMERICANS WHILE ATTENDING MOREHOUSE COLLEGE IN ATLANTA, GEORGIA.

MARTIN LUTHER KING JR.

ACTIVISM

The civil rights movement produced some of the greatest activists in history. Other local leaders also spoke out in their own communities and supported the movement. In the 1950s and 1960s, dozens of young African Americans convinced their peers to engage in peaceful protests against the racial inequality they faced every day. These demonstrations often took the form of **boycotts** or sit-ins.

Some of the most well-known sit-ins—a form of protest in which activists visit a place they're not allowed to be and refuse to leave—were organized not by national leaders such as King, but by college and high school students. Sit-ins to end segregation at businesses were an effective and nonviolent way to show support for the civil rights movement and bring change to the community.

THESE YOUNG AFRICAN AMERICANS STAGED A SIT-IN TO PROTEST SEGREGATION AT BROWN'S BASEMENT LUNCHEONETTE IN OKLAHOMA.

VICTORIES

The historic *Brown v. Board of Education of Topeka* decision was a major civil rights victory, and some lawmakers and school districts worked to begin integration immediately. However, the ruling only applied to public schools, and many people and districts resisted the court's decision. School segregation in some areas continued for many years.

In 1955, Rosa Parks refused to give her seat to a white man on a bus in Montgomery, Alabama. Her arrest prompted the Montgomery bus boycott, a large-scale, nonviolent protest of racially discriminatory laws in the South. This eventually led to a Supreme Court ruling that called for the desegregation of public transportation. Students holding sit-ins at lunch counters and other public spaces also continued to fight racial segregation. Many other smaller-scale civil rights victories took place in the late 1950s and early 1960s.

ROSA PARKS'S BRAVE REFUSAL TO ACCEPT A RACIST LAW LED MORE PEOPLE TO PROTEST SUCH LAWS.

THE MOTHER OF THE CIVIL RIGHTS MOVEMENT

Rosa Parks is widely famous for refusing to follow a racist law that required her to give up her seat. Before that incident, however, she was a major player in smaller civil rights protests. She was an officer at the NAACP in Montgomery for more than a decade before her famous arrest. After the Montgomery bus boycott and the Supreme Court decision calling for desegregation, she was highly regarded by African American activists for her bravery and leadership.

LOSSES

No matter how many victories the civil rights movement celebrated, many Americans continued to uphold racist ideals. Many civil rights leaders, such as King, were arrested and jailed. Thousands of protesters were beaten and **intimidated** by the police or racist groups such as the Ku Klux Klan.

Some young members of the civil rights movement were unhappy with the lack of change in the government. This led to rioting and violent protesting, which went against the mission of King's nonviolent civil rights movement. While King spoke against violence, other leaders, such as Malcolm X, said violence might be necessary. This caused the movement to split into different groups instead of working together.

The greatest loss for the civil rights movement, however, was the death of Martin Luther King Jr. in 1968.

STATUE OF MLK JR.

A POWERFUL LETTER

In 1963, Martin Luther King Jr. was arrested and jailed after his peaceful protest group was attacked by law enforcement in Birmingham, Alabama. While he was in prison, he wrote a letter explaining why he was fighting for civil rights and how his peaceful approach was the key to achieving equality. King's example is studied to this day as a perfect example of nonviolence and peaceful protesting, even in the face of dangerous opposition.

MALCOLM X WAS A CONVINCING SPEAKER AND CONTROVERSIAL LEADER. WHILE HE STOOD FOR CIVIL RIGHTS, HE SAID VIOLENCE MIGHT BE NEEDED TO OBTAIN THEM.

MALCOLM X

RISING POWER

One of the biggest accomplishments of the civil rights movement was the passage of the Voting Rights Act of 1965. Signed by President Lyndon B. Johnson after other laws had failed to protect African American voting rights, this act is meant to prevent local, state, and federal governments from denying anyone—regardless of race—the right to vote. However, some people challenged the Voting Rights Act, saying that it's unconstitutional.

Because the Voting Rights Act gave millions of African Americans a voice in politics, the number of African Americans in the government skyrocketed. This number has continued to increase into the 21st century. African Americans began electing politicians willing to fight for their rights, which has led to a greater sense of racial equality.

CONGRESS PASSED THE CIVIL RIGHTS ACT IN 1964. THIS ACT WAS MEANT TO END DISCRIMINATION AGAINST PEOPLE BASED ON RACE, RELIGION, OR WHICH COUNTRY THEY CAME FROM. HOWEVER, AFRICAN AMERICANS WERE STILL NOT SEEN AS EQUAL.

MODERN RESULTS

Since the passage of these landmark pieces of legislation, there has been improvement in civil rights, especially for African Americans. Since the passage of the Voting Rights Act, many African Americans have served in public offices at the local, state, and federal levels of the U.S. government.

In the 21st century, an African American rose to the nation's highest office. Barack Obama, who gained national attention as a senator from Illinois, served two terms as the nation's first African American president from 2009 to 2017. President Obama signed a number of pieces of legislation designed to further work toward an end to discrimination. One was the Frank R. Wolf International Religious Freedom Act, which allows people greater freedom to practice their religious beliefs openly.

BARACK OBAMA

JOHN LEWIS

HISTORIC MOMENTS

John Lewis, who was arrested and beaten for his role in the civil rights movement, has been a member of Congress since 1986.

BARACK OBAMA HAS BEEN AN INSPIRATION FOR AFRICAN AMERICANS AND POLITICIANS EVERYWHERE BECAUSE OF HIS LEADERSHIP AND SUCCESS.

DID IT SUCCEED?

While the civil rights movement resulted in reduced racial discrimination, a larger African American voting base, and a greater sense of equality across the United States, many have questioned whether it achieved its goals. While African Americans have more rights than they did in the 19th and 20th centuries, there is still widespread discrimination in American politics and society today.

Instead of looking at the civil rights movement as something that ended in the late 1960s, it's better to view it as a big step in the much larger process of creating a country in which everyone is treated equally. It's safe to say the civil rights movement was a successful step in the right direction toward a more equal United States.

ON AUGUST 28, 1963, MARTIN LUTHER KING JR. AND THOUSANDS OF OTHER CIVIL RIGHTS ACTIVISTS PARTICIPATED IN THE MARCH ON WASHINGTON FOR JOBS AND FREEDOM.

Marching for Freedom

The March on Washington for Jobs and Freedom was a peaceful protest of racial discrimination. Participants also marched to support civil rights legislation that was being discussed in Congress. One of the highlights of the march was Martin Luther King Jr.'s "I Have a Dream" speech, which he gave in front of the Lincoln Memorial in Washington, D.C.

TIMELINE

1865

The 13th Amendment is approved, bringing a legal end to slavery in the United States.

1896

The *Plessy v. Ferguson* case reaches the Supreme Court, which rules that "separate but equal" racial segregation is legal.

1909

Activists found the National Association for the Advancement of Colored People (NAACP). W. E. B. DuBois and Booker T. Washington emerge as African American leaders.

1954

The Supreme Court overturns *Plessy v. Ferguson* with its decision on *Brown v. Board of Education of Topeka*.

1955

Rosa Parks refuses to give her seat on a bus to a white man, which leads to the Montgomery bus boycott.

1965

Congress passes the Voting Rights Act.

1966

President Lyndon B. Johnson makes Robert C. Weaver the first African American member of a president's cabinet. Edward Brooke of Massachusetts is the first African American elected to the U.S. Senate by popular vote.

1967

Thurgood Marshall becomes the first African American justice of the U.S. Supreme Court.

2004

Barack Obama is elected as a senator for Illinois.

2009–2017

Barack Obama serves as president of the United States.

GLOSSARY

activist: Someone who acts strongly in support of or against an issue.

amendment: A change in the words or meaning of a law or document, such as a constitution.

boycott: A refusal to buy, use, or participate in something.

discriminate: To treat people unequally based on class, race, or religion.

emancipation: The act of setting someone free from control or slavery.

institution: A custom, practice, or law that is accepted and used by many people.

intimidate: To make someone afraid, especially by saying you'll do something to them in the future.

legislation: A law or set of laws made by a government.

minority: A group of people who are different from the larger group in a country or other area in some way, such as race or religion.

opposition: Acting or believing something different from someone else.

segregation: The separation of people based on race, class, or ethnicity.

INDEX

WEBSITES

Due to the changing nature of Internet links, PowerKids Press has developed an online list of websites related to the subject of this book. This site is updated regularly. Please use this link to access the list: www.powerkidslinks.com/kqah/civil